Mothers

We're nowhere without them

For my mother, who still has a sense of humour.

First published in the United Kingdom in 2015 by
Portico
43 Great Ormond Street
London
WC1N 3HZ

An imprint of Pavilion Books Company Ltd

ISBN 978-1-91023-210-1

A CIP catalogue record for this book is available from the British Library.

10 9 8 7 6 5

Design: Suzanne Perkins/grafica
Colour reproduction by Rival Colour Ltd, UK
Printed and bound by GPS Ltd, Slovenia
This book can be ordered direct from the publisher at www.pavilionbooks.com

THE WIT AND
Cath Tate
WISDOM OF

Mothers

We're nowhere without them

PORTICO

"Cheerleader, cash point, chauffeur, diplomat, pooper-scooper, waitress, short order cook, juice dispenser, sock matcher, climbing frame, referee, cuddly toy, encyclopaedia, damp shoulder, 24-hour medic, hotelier, dirty cup remover, purchasing manager, receptionist, bike mechanic, lost property attendant…

…just call me mother!"

"Baby?
What am I supposed to do
with a baby?"

"I have powers that can
  shorten the night."

"Mother does everything
by the book.

But I have other plans…"

"Life would be so much nicer if my mother would only stop knitting."

"Whatever it costs, this child is going to be a genius."

"…and we're signing her up for her doctorate next week."

Parenting is the process of passing all your faults on to your children.

"Parents do have a tendency to cramp one's style."

Children are a good substitute for people who have no pets.

The first half of your
life is ruined by
your parents,

the second half
by your children.

You need siblings to help you cope with parents.

"When no one's looking I'm going to sell him on eBay."

"*He* did it!"

"James, please get down off the shed,
your mother's here to collect you."

Motherhood is great once the children are asleep.

You know how old your children are by the size of their phone bill.

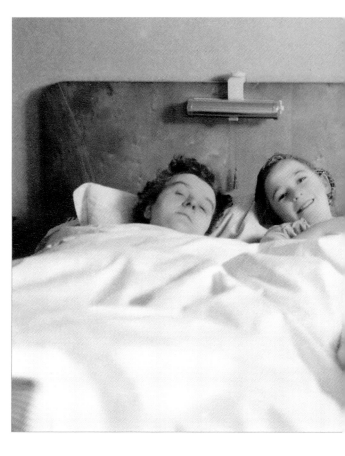

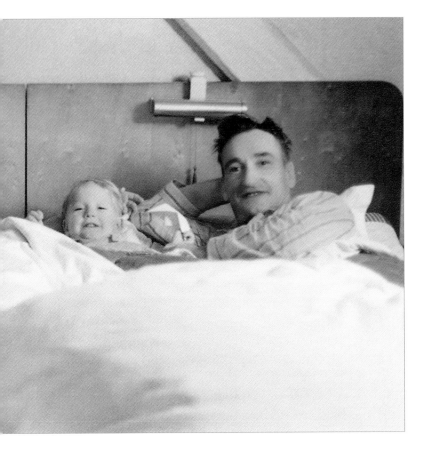

I childproofed the house but they keep getting back in.

Only children know what hard work parents are.

"My life seems to take up
all of my time."

Everyone knows mothers
have Super Powers.

"Wake me when the kids have grown up."

"Dinner *again*?
But I'm sure I fed them
yesterday!"

Behind every
exquisite meal someone
peels the potatoes.

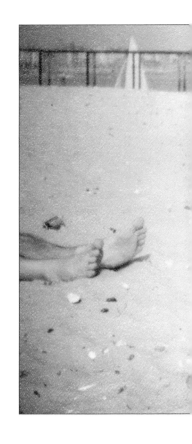

"Who needs lunch
   when there's plenty of
   sand to eat?"

"I believe banana is very good for the hair."

"I give my family a
choice of food:
1. Take it
2. Leave it."

Goddess
of the miraculously
refilling fridge.

The two great
questions in life:
1. How to achieve
self-awareness.
2. Who's going to
do the washing
up?

Mother's Taxi Service.
Available for:
ballet classes, karate
lessons, school runs,
football matches,

sleepovers, music lessons, parties, miscellaneous outings etc.
Reasonable rates apply.

For a few stolen moments she forgot she had any children.

Puberty is
when your parents start
turning really weird.

"No way am I going out
with my daughter dressed
like that!"

"No way am I going out
with my mother dressed
like that!"

Question Authority,
not your mother.

Mother refused to shop in places with loud music.

Apparently, even mother
was young once.

Every mother has the right
to embarrass her children.

"My daughter here has all the answers!"

"I *promise* I won't have
a party while you're away."

Only mother knows what's best for you.

"What's wrong with
your mother coming with
you on your gap year?"

Money isn't everything, but it keeps the kids in touch.

"If you make your home too comfortable, they'll never leave."

"It's not an empty nest
until I throw out the
kids' junk."

You should live
with your parents,

until you can move in
with your children.

Children are a
great comfort in
old age...

…and the quickest
way of getting
there.

Your mother can dish the dirt on the rest of the family…

...but of course her lips are sealed about you!

Never have children,
only grandchildren.

Grandparents are crucial
because parents haven't
got a clue.

The family is at the heart
of society…

…and mother is at the heart of the family.

However hard you try, you end up like your mother.

"Where would I be
without my mum?"

Cath Tate has lived and worked in London for more years than she cares to mention. She currently runs a greetings card company, Cath Tate Cards, with her daughter Rosie: the bulk of the photos and captions in this book started life as greetings cards.

The photos have been collected over the years by Cath and her friends in junk shops and vintage fairs. They are all genuine and show people in all their glory, on the beach, on a day out, posing stiffly for the photographer, drinking with friends, smiling or scowling at the camera.

The photographs were all taken sometime between 1880 and 1960. Times change but people, their friendships, their little joys and stupid mistakes, remain the same. Some things have changed though, and Cath Tate has used modern technical wizardry to tease some colour into the cheeks of those whose cheeks lost their colour some time ago.

The quotes that go with the photos come from random corners of life and usually reflect some current concern that is bugging her.

If you want to see all the current greetings cards and other ephemera available from Cath Tate Cards see www.cathtatecards.com

Cath Tate

Many thanks to all those helped me put this book together, including Discordia, who have fed me with wonderful photos and ideas over the years, and Suzanne Perkins, who has made sure everything looks OK, and also has a good line in jokes.

Picture credits

Photos from the collection of Cath Tate apart from the following:
Discordia/Simon: Pages 8–9, 12–13, 18–19, 22–23, 26–27, 34–35, 36–37, 40–41, 44–45, 60–61, 64–65, 66–67, 82–83, 92–93, 94–95, 102–103
Keith Allen: Pages 6–7, 20–21, 88–89, 110–111